ALTERNATOR
BOOKS™

MYSTERIES OF
STONEHENGE

Elizabeth Weitzman

Lerner Publications ◆ Minneapolis

For Eric and Eva

Lerner Publications Company
A division of Lerner Publishing Group, Inc.
241 First Avenue North
Minneapolis, MN 55401 USA

For reading levels and more information, look up this title at www.lernerbooks.com.

Main body text set in Aptifer Slab LT Pro Regular 11.5/18.
Typeface provided by Linotype AG.

Library of Congress Cataloging-in-Publication Data

Names: Weitzman, Elizabeth, author.
Title: Mysteries of Stonehenge / by Elizabeth Weitzman.
Description: Minneapolis : Lerner Publications, [2016] | Series: Ancient mysteries | Includes bibliographical references and index. | Audience: Grades 4–6.
Identifiers: LCCN 2016036195 (print) | LCCN 2016037191 (ebook) | ISBN 9781512440164 (lb : alk. paper) | ISBN 9781512449204 (eb pdf)
Subjects: LCSH: Stonehenge (England)—Juvenile literature. | Wiltshire (England)—Antiquities—Juvenile literature. | Megalithic monuments—England—Wiltshire—Juvenile literature.
Classification: LCC DA142 .W36 2016 (print) | LCC DA142 (ebook) | DDC 936.2/319—dc23

LC record available at https://lccn.loc.gov/2016036195

Manufactured in the United States of America
1-42278-26135-12/15/2016

TABLE OF CONTENTS

INTRODUCTION
SOLVING STONEHENGE

By summer of 2005, British archaeologist Mike Parker Pearson was extremely frustrated. He had been digging trenches near the massive rocks of Stonehenge in southwestern England for more than a year. He was determined to find the ancient remains of a prehistoric **settlement** near this five-thousand-year-old monument. So far, he'd come up empty.

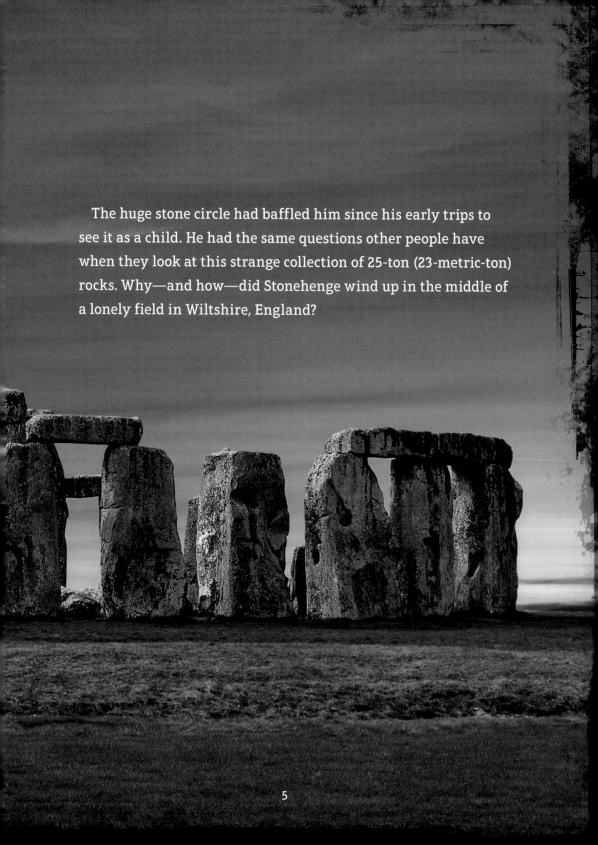

The huge stone circle had baffled him since his early trips to see it as a child. He had the same questions other people have when they look at this strange collection of 25-ton (23-metric-ton) rocks. Why—and how—did Stonehenge wind up in the middle of a lonely field in Wiltshire, England?

Parker Pearson had a thrilling theory. He thought the eerily isolated Stonehenge had actually been part of a bigger community. Unfortunately, though, he couldn't find any proof.

Mike Parker Pearson's 2005 research at Stonehenge was part of the Stonehenge Riverside Project, which lasted six years.

This drawing shows how a house at Durrington Walls might have looked around 3000 BCE.

And then everything changed. In August, Parker Pearson and his team began **excavating** a new patch of dirt. In an area called Durrington Walls, they discovered the remains of houses hidden underground for thousands of years.

Suddenly, we were all one step closer to understanding one of the great unsolved mysteries of the world.

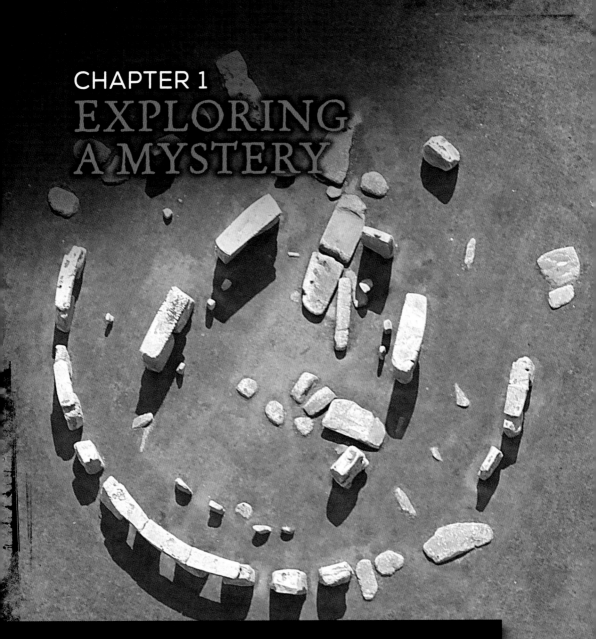

CHAPTER 1
EXPLORING A MYSTERY

A **henge** is what archaeologists call an ancient circle built on a bank of dirt with a ditch dug around it. Stonehenge is made of two kinds of stones: giant sandstones called sarsens and smaller igneous rocks known as bluestones.

Some of the stones are gone or fallen. But you can still imagine the original design. A wide circle of upright sarsen stones rings the outside, connected along the top by horizontal stones called **lintels**.

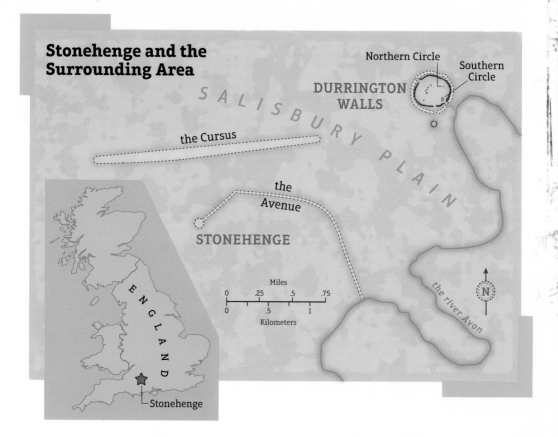

Stonehenge and the Surrounding Area

Northern Circle

Southern Circle

DURRINGTON WALLS

SALISBURY PLAIN

the Cursus

the Avenue

STONEHENGE

Miles
0   .25   .5   .75
0   .5   1
Kilometers

ENGLAND

Stonehenge

the river Avon

N

At the center sit five huge arches, arranged in a horseshoe shape. Each arch, or trilithon, is made of two standing sarsens and a lintel on top. Between the sarsens are the bluestones, arranged in another circle and semicircle.

In 2011 researchers found evidence that the grounds of Stonehenge had been used to honor the sun even before the stone structure was built.

ANCIENT SUN WORSHIP

Surrounded by earth and sky, Stonehenge looks as if it were dropped into the middle of nowhere. But the stones were placed very carefully. On the longest day of the year, the **summer solstice**, the sun rises just above the Heel Stone, a sarsen outside the entrance of Stonehenge. And on the shortest day, the **winter solstice**, the sun sets directly between the largest trilithon.

Thousands of years after Stonehenge was built, it still has the power to amaze. Everyone who sees the sun rise over the Heel Stone or set between the trilithon is awed by its beauty. In fact, many archaeologists believe that Stonehenge was designed to honor the sun.

Most of Stonehenge was constructed during a period of early human history known as the late **Neolithic** era. This was the last part of the Stone Age, around 3000 BCE. But it wasn't finished until centuries later, around 2000 BCE, during the more advanced Bronze Age.

If you wanted to build a massive structure in the twenty-first century, you might gather engineers, architects, materials, and equipment. But Stonehenge was created long before modern technology or machinery existed.

MAGIC THEORIES

How was Stonehenge built? No one knows for sure.
But people have come up with lots of theories over the
years. Back in the twelfth century, a writer named
Geoffrey of Monmouth started the popular legend that
the wizard Merlin used magic to steal the stones from
giants in Ireland. Another myth is more believable.
In the seventeenth century, an archaeologist named
John Aubrey suggested that Stonehenge was a temple
built by ancient priests called druids. Then another
archaeologist named William Stukeley publicly agreed
with him. Both men were well respected, so people
were quick to believe their ideas.

One historical myth suggests
that giants moved the stones
and built Stonehenge. Do
you think that's more likely
than aliens building it?

The truth is that the original druids arrived in England hundreds of years after Stonehenge was already built. Did they ever visit the site? Maybe. They didn't leave written records, so they remain almost as mysterious as Stonehenge itself.

MYTH ALERT!
Some people have said that ancient aliens came to Earth to create Stonehenge. According to this theory, extraterrestrials used the circle as a landing spot for their spaceship. They also supposedly built the Egyptian pyramids and the stone statues of Easter Island while they were here. But scientists have never found any evidence to support this idea.

Druids have also been described as magicians who worshipped nature. The circle certainly *feels* as if it has a magical bond with nature. That may be why it's still associated with druids. In fact, you can see people who call themselves modern-day druids if you visit Stonehenge during a solstice.

CHAPTER 2

AN ANCIENT COMMUNITY

This illustration, published in the nineteenth century, shows one artist's idea of Neolithic life at Stonehenge.

When Parker Pearson and his team discovered those underground houses in 2005, they proved that people really had lived at Durrington Walls. The location of Stonehenge may not have been as random as everyone once believed.

At 42 acres (17 hectares), Durrington Walls was the biggest community of its time in the area. In fact, it may have held as many as a thousand houses.

What did people do there? No one knows for sure, but we can find hints in three big circles made of wood. Scientists have found large numbers of animal bones around the circles. This suggests the circles were used as a gathering place, perhaps for feasts and other celebrations of the solstices.

MYTH ALERT!

Stonehenge is aligned, or lined up, with the sun in a very specific way. Archaeologists have also noticed unusual alignments with stars and the moon. That led some people to think builders used the monument to predict lunar eclipses and the movement of the stars. Scientists have proven that the alignments are not actually very precise. So it's unlikely that this was the creators' intention. But the monument *could* have been a giant celestial observatory, or place to look at the sky.

CELEBRATING THE CIRCLE OF LIFE

Between Stonehenge and Durrington Walls sits another monument called the Cursus. This is a big stretch of land nearly 2 miles (3.2 kilometers) long. At one end is a burial ground.

By looking at the human remains buried near Stonehenge, archaeologists can learn about the people who once lived there. For example, certain bones look different in men, women, and children. Because we know that many women were buried in the area, we can guess that they played important roles in their society. Perhaps they were political rulers or religious leaders.

Scientists think that the heavy stones of Stonehenge may have represented death. Modern gravestones are used for the same purpose. If that's true, then why were the circles at Durrington Walls made of wood? Perhaps wood represented life for the builders. The Cursus may have helped separate the land for the living (Durrington Walls) and the land for the dead (Stonehenge).

Keep in mind that Neolithic people probably saw death as part of the human experience. It wasn't something to fear but an event to respect in a special way.

One fascinating clue the Stonehenge Riverside Project found was the remains of a Neolithic house.

We can imagine that on the morning of the summer solstice, the community gathered at Stonehenge. As the sun rose over the Heel Stone, they had a ceremony to honor and perhaps bury their ancestors. As the day continued, they traveled along a path called Stonehenge Avenue, down to the river Avon. By nightfall, they were back at Durrington Walls for a huge feast.

In the winter, they turned the trip around. They began the day at the Southern Circle in Durrington Walls. They ended it by watching the sun set at Stonehenge.

We're getting closer to a possible *why* of Stonehenge. For the people who built it, this extraordinary place may have represented the connection between summer and winter, life and death, and the heavens and Earth.

Modern druids celebrate nature's cycles at Stonehenge.

DIG DEEP!

In 2002 archaeologists found the grave of a Bronze Age skeleton *(below)* near Stonehenge. Pottery, gold hair ornaments, and copper knives in his grave suggest he was rich and powerful. He also had so many arrowheads that the archaeologists nicknamed him the Amesbury Archer.

Tests on his teeth showed he had traveled a long way, possibly from Germany. And he had many injuries, including a missing kneecap. This helps support the popular theory that people went to Stonehenge to be magically healed.

Knowing more about Durrington Walls also helps us understand *how* Stonehenge was built. If you have thousands of people inspired by a special location, you have thousands of hands ready to build a monument there.

We don't know for sure how people built Stonehenge. But it is likely that they worked together to use simple machines, such as levers and wedges.

We know the sarsens of Stonehenge came from about 20 miles (32 km) away. And the bluestones came all the way from Wales, 180 miles (290 km) away. These rocks are *massive*. Each bluestone weighs about 4 tons (3.6 metric tons). The largest sarsens are 30 feet (9.1 meters) tall and weigh about 40 tons (36 metric tons) each. That's the size of a small house! So how did the stones wind up in Salisbury Plain, the flat area of land where Stonehenge sits?

Some historians think Ice Age glaciers carried the bluestones from Wales to an area near Salisbury Plain. But other scientists believe it's more likely that large communities worked together to move them. People might have lifted the rocks on rollers made of logs and then pushed them to the site. They also could have used oxen to pull them or handmade rafts to float them down the river.

ANTLER CLUES

In the 1920s, an excavation at Stonehenge turned up pieces of deer antlers. These have turned out to be a huge help in modern times. By using a technique called **radiocarbon dating**, scientists can figure out how old the antlers are. And that can tell us when the monuments were made.

DIG DEEP!

Radar technology allows archaeologists to scan beneath the ground without having to dig it up. In 2015 radar technology led to an amazing discovery: a giant collection of stones that has been buried at Durrington Walls for thousands of years. The stones are 3 feet (0.9 m) underground, part of a row that was five times as big as Stonehenge! Not only that, but these stones were aligned with the sun during the solstice.

Scientists believe ancient people used antlers, wood, and smaller rocks to shape the stones and fit them together. To place the stones in deep holes in the ground, the builders may have used huge piles of earth as ramps and long wooden poles as levers. Using ropes made from strips of bark, many people working together could have lifted the stones upright.

Archaeologists found this piece of broken deer antler in a Stonehenge excavation. Radiocarbon dating tells us it was used around 3000 BCE.

This would have been incredibly slow, difficult, and dangerous work. So it's no surprise that it took around fifteen hundred years from the first phase of building to the last.

CHAPTER 4
PRESERVING HISTORY

Eventually, the Stone Age turned into the Bronze Age and later the Industrial or Modern Age. Travelers started coming to Britain from across Europe. They brought new tools, new ideas, and new ways of life. They found new ways to celebrate the rituals of life and death.

Over time, Stonehenge started falling into disrepair. Anyone could walk right up and touch the rocks. Some people even chipped off pieces to take home. By the middle of the twentieth century, highways were cutting through Salisbury Plain. Stonehenge gained some protection, though, when it was made an official World Heritage Site in 1986.

Modern tourists must stay at least 10 yards (9.1 m) from the rocks at Stonehenge. There are no restrooms or other modern buildings within a mile (1.6 km) of the site.

MODERN STONEHENGE

These days, a British charity called English Heritage keeps Stonehenge safe from the impact of modern life. Threats from tourism, climate change, and construction are all watched carefully. Anyone who wants to build or excavate near the area must get permission.

Every year, nearly a million people visit Stonehenge. Tourists used to lean against, write on, or climb up the rocks. Now they have to stay behind a rope fence.

But there are still two great chances to see

The winter solstice
at Stonehenge

At the summer solstice, people celebrate seventeen hours of daylight with music, drumming, and dancing into the night.

Stonehenge up close every year: the summer and winter solstices. The rope is lifted on these special days. And thousands of strangers stand together, right inside the stone circles, to watch the sun rise or set.

With the bright rays brilliantly shining through the great trilithon, modern-day visitors might as well be transported back to 2300 BCE. The world has changed immeasurably since then. But twice a year, we can still experience the magic that inspired our Neolithic ancestors.

SCIENCE SPOTLIGHT
RADIOCARBON DATING

How do archaeologists date Stonehenge? One method is by using radiocarbon dating, also called carbon dating, or carbon-14 dating. Every living thing, or organism, contains particles of a chemical element called carbon. Some of these particles are radioactive. When an organism dies, the carbon begins to decay at a very specific rate. So we can figure out how old a fossil is by measuring how much radiocarbon is left within it. At Stonehenge, archaeologists have tested antler pieces (below) and buried bones to determine the age of the stones around them.

Timeline

3500 BCE	The Stonehenge Cursus and other early monuments are created.
3000–2935	The first stage of Stonehenge building, including a large earth bank surrounded by a deep ditch, begins.
2640–2480	The second stage of building occurs. Neolithic people settle in Durrington Walls. People bring sarsens and bluestones to the Stonehenge site and put them in place.
2480–2280	In the third stage of building, the avenue that connects Stonehenge to the river Avon is completed.
2280–1520	During the fourth, fifth, and sixth stages of building, the stones are rearranged, and more pits and ditches are dug.
1136 CE	Geoffrey of Monmouth writes the first legends about Stonehenge in *The History of the Kings of Britain*.
1666	John Aubrey is one of the first archaeologists to research the area.
1986	Stonehenge is declared a World Heritage Site.
2003–2009	Mike Parker Pearson and the Stonehenge Riverside Project excavate the land around Stonehenge, including Durrington Walls.
2015	The Stonehenge Hidden Landscapes Project finds remains of a monument five times the size of Stonehenge.

GLOSSARY

excavating: digging in the earth in search of buried remains

henge: a prehistoric monument made of a round bank of earth and a surrounding ditch

lintels: blocks that sit across the tops of two standing columns

Neolithic: from the late Stone Age, roughly between 10,000 and 2000 BCE

radiocarbon dating: a scientific method used to determine how old a fossil is

settlement: a place where people have built a new community

summer solstice: the longest day of the year, when the sun rises to its most northern point in the sky. The summer solstice is always on or around June 21.

winter solstice: the shortest day of the year, when the sun rises to its southernmost point in the sky. The winter solstice is always on or around December 21.

FURTHER INFORMATION

Aronson, Marc, and Mike Parker Pearson. *If Stones Could Speak: Unlocking the Secrets of Stonehenge.* Washington, DC: National Geographic, 2010.

BBC Bitesize: What Is Stonehenge?
http://www.bbc.co.uk/guides/zg8q2hv

English Heritage: Stonehenge
http://www.english-heritage.org.uk/visit/places/stonehenge/history/#

Manning, Mick. *The Secrets of Stonehenge.* London: Frances Lincoln Children's Books, 2013.

McDaniel, Sean. *Stonehenge.* Minneapolis: Bellwether Media, 2012.

National Geographic: Stonehenge Photos
http://science.nationalgeographic.com/science/archaeology/photos/stonehenge/#/stonehenge-dusk_24763_600x450.jpg

Richards, Jon, and Ed Simkins. *Record-Breaking Building Feats.* Minneapolis: Hungry Tomato, 2016.

"Was Stonehenge Built for Prehistoric Rock Music?"
http://teachingkidsnews.com/2014/03/16/1-stonehenge-built-prehistoric-rock-music

INDEX

PHOTO ACKNOWLEDGMENTS

The images in this book are used with the permission of: © Gordan/Shutterstock.com (grunge border texture); © Paul Lampard/Dreamstime.com, p. 1; © Raduang/Dreamstime.com, p. 4; Adam Stanford © Aerial-Cam Ltd., pp. 6, 17, 23, 28; © Sano, Kazuhiko/National Geographic Creative/Bridgeman Images, p. 7; London Aerial/Photoshot/Newscom, p. 8; © Laura Westlund/Independent Picture Service, p. 9; © Markus Gann/Dreamstime.com, p. 10; © Look and Learn/Bridgeman Images, p. 11; Adam Woolfitt/robertharding/Newscom, p. 12; Album/Newscom, p. 14; Hulteng KRT/Newscom, p. 16; © 1000 Words/Shutterstock.com, pp. 18, 27; © Salisbury Museum/Bridgeman Images, p. 19; © Chris Clor/Blend Images/Alamy, p. 20; © De Agostini Picture Library/Bridgeman Images, p. 21; © Hel080808/Dreamstime.com, p. 24; © Victor Maschek/Shutterstock.com, p. 25; © Stonehenge, Winter Solstice (photo)/Salisbury, Wiltshire, UK/Bridgeman Images, p. 26.

Front cover: © Paul Lampard/Dreamstime.com (Stonehenge image); © Gordan/Shutterstock.com (grunge border texture).